T0208223

*Life...*As I See It!

Quotes to Live by and Ponder

Jeffrey C. Wickey, Sr.

iUniverse, Inc.
Bloomington

iUniverse books may be ordered through booksellers or by contacting:

iUniverse
1663 Liberty Drive
Bloomington, IN 47403
www.iuniverse.com
1-800-Authors (1-800-288-4677)

Because of the dynamic nature of the Internet, any web addresses or links
contained in this book may have changed since publication and may no
longer be valid. The views expressed in this work are solely those of the
author and do not necessarily reflect the views of the publisher, and the
publisher hereby disclaims any responsibility for them.

Any people depicted in stock imagery provided by Thinkstock are
models, and such images are being used for illustrative purposes only.

Certain stock imagery © Thinkstock.

ISBN: 978-1-4502-9388-4 (sc)
ISBN: 978-1-4502-9387-7 (ebook)

Library of Congress Control Number: 2011901454

Printed in the United States of America

iUniverse rev. date: 02/17/2011

Acknowledgements

I'd like to express a very special thank you to my lovely wife, Ellen, who has stuck by her anxiety-ridden and adventure-driven husband for the past 31 years. I honestly know of no better person on the face of this planet, and I love her more than mere words could ever express. Thanks for sharing this earthbound experience with me!

I'd like to recognize and thank my son, JJ, and daughter, Laura, for their support, patience, and understanding while following dad around the world on his military assignments. I know it wasn't easy for either of you at times and for that I apologize.

To my little sister, Lisa, a Seattle-based photographer, and her husband Chris, thank you for helping me keep my mind open and cup half full. With you two on my side, all things are possible!

Lastly, I'd also like to thank the countless individuals I've known over the years in the military, government, and corporate arenas. Regardless of the experience, I've managed to learn a little something from all of you.

Introduction

I've always enjoyed reading quotations from famous people and great leaders. At many times in my life, their words of wisdom have not only provided me with inspiration and motivation, but have guided me through some very tough and challenging times.

I've learned many lessons in the course of my military and civilian careers, as well as through meeting and interacting with countless people in the course of my travels. As such, I wanted to document some of my thoughts and realizations on life (as a result of my lessons learned) so that my children and future grandchildren might benefit from my words and guidance long after I am gone. I hope the words contained within these pages resonate with them (and other readers) and make them think deeply about their lives, the lives of others, and the world around them…of which they are, and will be, an integral and important part. So, in a sense, this book is my legacy to them.

All the quotes in this book are mine and are based solely on my personal and professional experiences, observations, and encounters over the past 30 years. As such, they represent my thoughts and the way I interpret and view the world around me.

Lastly, as much of what I've learned over the last three decades has come from trial and error and the school of hard knocks, I hope others are able to benefit from the lessons I've learned, as well. If my words can help but one person, then I consider myself and this book a resounding success.

We are all a continuous work in progress. The things we learn, the experiences we have, and even the books we read shape our minds and mold our beings into what we are today and to what we will become in the future. Sad is the person who does not realize the value of education and life-long learning, who fails to step outside their comfort zone and experience new things, and who does not pick up a book every now and then.

A person who sees only through their own eyes sees far less than the person who is able to see through the eyes of others.

Most people spend an inordinate amount of time and effort worrying about what they cannot do and inventing creative excuses as to why they cannot do it. If an equal amount of time and effort was spent considering the possibilities of what they can do or might be able to accomplish, their lives would undoubtedly proceed in a drastically different direction.

As human beings, we live in various spheres of responsibility. Whether it is the family sphere, the community sphere, or the global sphere, whichever we are engaged in at the moment determines where our focus should be and our responsibilities lie.

A word is just a word, a thought just a thought, until it is expressed in some fashion. At that point it becomes either an asset or a potential liability. Therefore, it is important to choose every spoken and written word carefully.

Avoid bringing the pains of the past into the present. It serves absolutely no purpose but to poison the mind and divert your focus from what is certainly more important, relevant, and within your control…your future.

Seasons come and seasons go. We too shall pass as the seasons, not knowing which will be our last.

A complainer who is focused on finding a solution to remedy the source of the complaint can be the impetus for great change.

Be aware…you can learn as much from observing a person doing something wrong as you can from observing a person doing something right.

A word to the wise…listening to others can be the wisest endeavor you'll ever undertake.

The path to enlightenment is often wrought with great misfortune, pain, and immense struggle. Reaching the end of the path in the course of a lifetime comes to but a few. Those few are the true heroes of our earthly existence.

To mentor one young person is to benefit many.

I am grateful to those individuals who settle for mediocrity, or less, for they have made it easier for me to get ahead and prosper.

To be truly fulfilled in life, one must see their soul's purpose in the distance and then drive like hell to reach it. More often than not, though, you'll be the only one in the car.

Living in the past stunts your growth.

At one point or another, I have been let down by
nearly every human being I know. Fortunately, my
loyal and loving dog allows me to continue seeing
the world with eyes of hope and compassion.

As they say, an object in motion tends to stay in motion
and an object at rest stays at rest. Which one best sums
up your life…an object on the move or an object at rest?

It is beyond the realm of the conscious mind
to see ourselves as perfect human beings.
As such, perfection is a goal pursued by the
irrational as opposed to the rational mind.

Don't spend your time worrying about gaining respect from others. Simply, set lofty goals and work hard to reach them. By doing so, you will not only garner respect along the way, but, more importantly, you will learn to respect yourself, which is far more important in the long run.

Rest if you must…while others pass you by.

Man's imperfections keep life interesting…
to say the least. After all, if it were not for other's imperfections and shortcomings to compare against, how would we gauge ourselves?

Take great care not to lose your way on the long and winding road. Remember that the shortest, most direct road is rarely the most rewarding.

Shortcuts usually come with a price.

In our society, far more attention is given to those who can effectively speak verses those who can effectively listen. This is unfortunate because when was the last time you were actually conned or bullshitted by a good listener?

The road to success is rarely a straight and predictable journey. Rather, it is one full of stop lights, roundabouts, and dead ends.

The next time you see an American flag flying high, stop and reflect on what it stands for, and be sure to give a special thank you to those who have served and died so you and yours wouldn't have to.

The forced distribution of hard earned wealth to those unwilling to work is unjust and can only be viewed by the rational mind as nothing less than criminal extortion.

Many people spend their entire lives confined to the valley because it is beautiful, familiar, and safe. However, when you gain the courage to look up at the mountain and wonder what it would be like to stand on top of it, your life will never be the same. The climb out of the familiar and the trek into the unknown will open your eyes and mind to wondrous new adventures.

The term "leader" is perhaps one of the most misunderstood and bastardized terms in the American lexicon. As a result, most people are thrust into the role ill-prepared, not fully understanding the fundamentals, gravity, or the wide swath of responsibility that accompanies the role.

When it comes to government-provided assistance (welfare), governments need to determine and enforce a more effective means to distinguish between those who are unwilling to work and those who are incapable of working. Providing perpetual hand outs to those who deceptively subsist on the success of others, or see it as "okay" to take from others while giving nothing to society in return, only serves to preserve the welfare state as a growth industry.

Your life can either be a blessing or a curse. The choice is absolutely yours and yours alone.

Your elected official can be your best friend or your worst enemy. The problem is you never fully see a person's true colors, or their secret motives revealed, until after he or she is elected.

Always try first to find a solution to your problem before reaching out to others for help. The fastest and surest way of reaching a level of self-sufficiency is through exercising your own ingenuity, resourcefulness, and judgment. This is God's way of instilling confidence and nature's way of ensuring survival of the fittest.

The trouble with politics is that it's full of politicians who believe, foremost, in self-preservation and not "courageous citizens" who are truly committed to the betterment of our nation and its people…often at their own expense.

With "power" comes an understanding of good will, restraint, respect, compromise, and self. At least it should.

The best (most rewarding) win is the one you acquire as a direct result of your own abilities and preparations.

When it's all said and done, and we're off to meet out maker, all we can hope to leave behind of real significance is the love and respect we've earned from our family and friends. All else matters not one iota in the grand scheme of things and will begin to fade away as soon as the first shovel of dirt is tossed upon us.

We can give love and we can be loved. However, it is the truly fortunate man or woman who perfects and sustains both simultaneously.

Give a man something and he will be satisfied. Make him earn it and he will be fulfilled.

Children are both a challenge and a blessing. But they are a challenge and a blessing of our choosing. How we deal with either conveys our character and maturity.

The value of a quiet moment to the human psyche is immeasurable.

Rest only long enough to replenish your physical and psychological being. Too much rest is detrimental to your physical and mental capabilities and counterproductive to achieving your goals and dreams.

We wish, we wish, we wish…then, sadly, we lay on our deathbeds disappointed we didn't act upon those wishes while we had the chance.

Opportunities come and go, often unnoticed to the undisciplined eye. The disciplined eye is always on guard to see what others do not, and to recognize and grab the right opportunity as it dashes by…never to pass by again.

Your destiny does not wait for you while you squander away the hours with silly, non-productive activities.

We live to love and we love to live. Blessed is the man who experiences both with passion and zest.

Desire only gets us so far. It's enthusiasm and fortitude, mixed with a hefty dose of desire, that separates the men from the boys and determines who will succeed and who will fail.

The immense power of concentrated thought is only superseded by the power of focused and persistent action on behalf of that thought.

Why does man always wonder why? Hmmm…

Thank God for the person who can say it all in a nutshell!

Opportunities to learn lie in wait around every corner and with every step we take, whether forward or backward. Ironically, often the most important and enduring learning experiences come from the steps we take backwards. Only in hindsight, though, do they become apparent…at least for most of us.

Man only learns to the limits of his needs and desires.

Not every person receives the love they deserve, which is sad, because every person is capable of generating and giving more love than they know what to do with.

The educated show their ignorance when they believe only they can have good ideas.

Coffee makes the world go around…
albeit a bit faster than we would like.

A person who thinks before speaking
is one wise son-of-a-bitch.

Ideas can come from anywhere and anyone
and at anytime…and often do.

One person + another person = 2. However, a man and a woman = 3. And that's what keeps mankind from extinction. Let us never forget our simple math.

Music is sustenance for the soul and fuel for man's spirit.

Ideas are to be nourished and cared for as the most delicate of infants.

The soul is not 5'1" or 6'5". It is unbound by physical dimension, which means that we must learn to live and thrive beyond our physical selves.

Everything in life requires balance. For example, when the gap between the "haves" and the "have-nots" grows beyond the fine line that divides them, men will move mountains to bring it back to what they perceive is the proper sense of balance...if not equilibrium.

The ability to see and appreciate the significance of the moment as it is occurring is perhaps the most valuable trait a leader can hope to acquire.

History has a tendency to repeat itself time and time again. Yet, man always seems to believe that what happened in the past is irrelevant to the present tense and that we are somehow superior to our predecessors. As such, history is doomed to repeat itself time and time again.

Recently, it seems to me that Congress maintains the following viewpoint: In light of the current situation, we have no choice but to put your future on hold. At least until we can figure out what the hell we're doing and are able to determine what future we deem appropriate for you.

It is theoretically possible that we, as a species, could expire at any moment. Even with this realization, we continue to march on as though…

Dream, dream, and dream. And when you're done…dream some more. At some point, though, pick one dream and pursue it with all your vigor. Otherwise, the day will certainly come when you will be incapable of reaching any of them.

I might be tired, but I cannot show it, as others will take advantage of the opportunity to kick it up a notch and pass me by.

The uninformed man matters little in the grand scheme of things.

The leader who thinks of himself or herself as a great leader probably isn't. Greatness is an attribute bestowed upon you by others, not given to yourself.

It is okay to pat yourself on the back. In fact, I believe it is healthy to do so. Just be careful not to do it too loudly, or in public.

If, for whatever reason, you are unable to march to your own drummer, then certainly march to the drummer nearest your own ideals.

The meek shall inherit the world only when
they overcome their meekness.

Never, never, never give up…until your time
is up. Then, it's okay to concede and rest.

Do not willingly succumb to the thoughts or whims
of others without first checking with Mr. Reason.

A man can only achieve manhood if he is allowed to be a man. And when society finally figures out what a man is supposed to be, I hope it's announced loudly from the highest mountains, skyscrapers, and grain elevators they can find.

Whine if you must. Just do it quietly so the rest of us can figure out a solution to your problem.

Knowledge is an attribute we all possess regardless of our level of education or range of travel. Even if you were born and raised in a cave, you have knowledge of the cave, which is certainly of value to someone other than yourself.

You have never been fully "alive" until your life has been in danger of ending with a moment's notice.

The depth of a loyal dog's eyes can melt the toughest of men.

Most likely there is someone searching for what you already know and take for granted.

Communicating is easy in theory, yet surprisingly difficult in practice. It's at the moment when thoughts and words start to exchange that things gets a little dicey.

I could never live just for today as it is the possibilities of tomorrow that excite me and drive me forward.

Never make the mistake of assuming others know what you know…or know something to the depth of your understanding.

The mind can never be fully understood…let alone harnessed. And thank God for that.

The thing with marriage is that the dreams and expectations going in are about as lofty and ideal as they're going to get. If they weren't, no one would ever get married.

The success of an organization is in direct correlation to the level of knowledge it possesses. The longevity of an organization's success, however, is in direct correlation to the knowledge its members share.

Marriage is like dollar cost averaging. You frequently invest as much as you can and over the long haul the high points and low points will balance each other out keeping things on an even keel. The key is the steady, disciplined, and willingly equal investment by both parties. That…and a hell of a lot of luck.

I would venture to say that nearly all marriages are ignorantly myopic in the beginning, which is probably by God's design. If we were all looking ahead to the trials and tribulations that lie ahead, few would be willing to board the ship and take the journey. Only the most adventurous of souls would accept the challenges and risks of sailing into the unknown.

There are few things more tragic and detrimental to an organization's well being than the knowledge it loses to ignorance or neglect.

Why would anyone wish misfortune upon another person except for the sole purpose of making themselves feel better about their own insecurities?

The human race has not evolved as far as we would like to believe it has. We've just used our superior intellect to elevate our basic animal instincts to a much higher and more destructive level of existence.

No human being can be omnipresent in the physical sense. Despite advances in technology, we can still only occupy one minuscule place on Earth at a time…much to our chagrin.

Man can only be comfortable…and
fully satisfied…when he is dead.

The happiest man is the one who is content with his
lot in life and is fulfilled by the simplest of things.

People fail to grasp the immense power that can
be generated by the collective and concentrated
movement of the masses. If this power was ever
realized, harnessed, and put into action, no creation
of man, government, or otherwise, could withstand
its force. The problem lies with finding the spark
required to stir and mobilize such a force.

The most beautiful view a man can ever aspire
to behold is the love in his wife's eyes. All other
majesties in the world pale in comparison.

It's the year 2011 and man feels as aimless, confused,
and uncertain of his future as perhaps he ever has
before. Yet, we pride ourselves on how far we've
come as an evolved and superior species.

If man's innate desire was to be alone, we'd all be
doing it. As it is not, with few exceptions, we find our
measure and comfort in the presence of others.

Trying to understand others in relationship to our own existence would be easier if we first understood ourselves. However, as I don't believe we can ever really understand our own depths, I guess we'll never really be able to truly understand anyone else's either.

In life, we learn more through our relationships with others than by any other means. Therefore, your future success or failure depends, to a great degree, on the relationships you form and the company you allow into your life.

Ideally, each person should measure themselves according to their own accomplishments and not to the measure given to them by others, or by the accomplishments of others.

If I had to articulate one thing that, if everyone would do, would make the world a better place, it would be, "Make kindness a habit". In other words, exhibitions of kindness should be the norm, rather than the exception in our lives.

If you want to be remembered fondly, give of yourself without expectation of return or reward.

Life is a race against time. The only obstacles preventing you from reaching the finish line are you and the insecurities you decide to carry along with you.

Giving love and kindness is like playing sports. The more you practice them, the easier they become.

If so few of us relish the thought of dying, then why do we consistently make choices that hasten our demise?

If we had to pay our hard-earned money for all the emotional baggage we carry with us through life, we'd be shedding bags so fast it would make our heads spin.

If, it seems, time is always of the essence,
then what is the true essence of time?

Being "somewhere" is not the same as "being there".
In other words, we can physically occupy a certain
place at a certain time, while the mind, having its own
agenda, might be off somewhere else all together. The
ability to align the agendas of the body and mind so
that they habitually intersect in the right place at the
right time is the key to success in everything we do.

Each of us is relevant in the proper context.

To merely exist and flow effortlessly with the currents of life, I believe, is counter to what God intended for our earthly experience. Therefore, to really "live" as God intended, we must occasionally seek out the rough, unpathed roads, for that is where the true treasures of life lie waiting for us.

There is nothing more exciting and rewarding as the thrill of discovery. If discovery was an art form, I'd desire to be an artist. If discovery was a profession, I'd desire to be an expert in that field of study.

There is a place of acceptance and comfort for all of us. Unfortunately, it just might be in the place we have yet to look. So don't give up looking.

A true friend willingly stands by you when no one else is willing to…and has your back when others are backing away.

A good rule of thumb is not to speak for ten seconds after a thought enters your head. If after ten seconds it still seems applicable and relevant to the moment, then say it, albeit with brevity and tact.

Our strengths and weaknesses are God's way of helping us select the right path when we reach the proverbial "Y" in the road.

Are we all so blind that we cannot see politics for what it really is…an elaborate reward for the egotistical narcissist and a pulpit for those ignorant to the plight of the common citizen?

We should rejoice in everything that stimulates our senses, regardless of how pleasing the experience.

Amazingly, many people seem to think the solution to a problem is to run from it or deny it exists altogether. Using denial or seeking refuge from your own doubts and insecurities is not the answer. In fact, with each passing day the problem will only get bigger. Better to deal with it early while it is still manageable.

To understand rock and roll is to appreciate
the very essence of the big bang that created
the universe…only with electric guitars.

Rock and roll isn't necessarily the best thing
in life…but it is certainly in the top two.

There can be no equality of men until man is able to see
others reflecting his own image in every characteristic
and attribute. If one hair is out of place, if there is one
blemish on the skin, man will seize upon that difference
and exploit it to the fullest of his perceived benefit.

Receiving is not a prerequisite for giving.

If you have to be told to give of yourself in
a relationship, then the point is moot.

The last thing you will experience on Earth, if you are
lucky, is the love you have sown during your lifetime.

Taking advantage of those that give to others
is about as devilish an act as I can fathom.

You will be perceived by others in
accordance to the way you allow.

The uneducated person is the pawn the
educated use to seed their ambitions.

You don't have to be all things to all people, nor should you. Just be true to yourself and surround yourself with people who understand you and appreciate you for who you are. Buggers to the rest.

Read and learn...or suffer among the minions.

The primary question each of us should be asking ourselves on a daily basis is, "Am I doing my absolute best?" If you can answer "yes" to that question, then you are a success in God's eyes.

Man is so incredibly stubborn that he refuses to take notice of impending danger even when it's about to slap him in the face? As a result, he does not heed the urgency of the situation until it is too late to respond intelligently. Then, he is overcome with sorrow and regret, asking how this could have happened, how can it be prevented in the future, and, most importantly, who is to blame.

Some people are so prideful they refuse to accept help when it is offered, regardless of how desperate their situation might be. How sad it is to confuse pride with ignorance and stubbornness.

As a leader, decisiveness is critically important. It is often better to make a decision based on the knowledge and insight you have available at the moment, than it is to not make a decision at all or wait for information that might never come.

The strength of a man's muscles is no match
for the strength of a man's spirit.

The true test of a man is how he accepts and deals with
responsibility when it is thrust upon him unprepared.

Sport plays a vital function in our society, because it
focuses our natural tendencies of aggression and warfare in
a way that keeps the general populace diverted and at bay.

In no way, shape, or form is it ever acceptable
to talk down to or belittle another person.

Do not ever look down upon others for you can
never be high enough in stature or appointment that
someone won't be looking down upon you in return.

There comes a time when every person must
make a decision. Do I value myself more than I
value others? That critically important decision
drives the future of your existence here on
Earth as well as your place in the afterlife.

The degree of respect you earn in life
is in direct proportion to the degree of
effort it has taken you to earn it.

You don't have to receive love to give love.
Therefore, give your love unconditionally and you
will be all the better for it…as will the world.

Never stop believing that goodness shall
overcome evil or you will give evil the upper
hand in the battle for your soul.

See the man who has nothing and feel for him, for one day you might find yourself staring at his reflection in the mirror.

Even the most powerful and wealthiest of men cannot buy another person's trust. Given the choice of money, possessions, or trust, I'll take trust hands down, because it's the hardest, most elusive commodity on Earth to acquire and maintain.

Seeking the truth in our government's actions is a cause we all should be willing to pursue. If everything is on the up and up, then there should be nothing to hide.

Doubt the man who cannot look you squarely in the eyes.

The unemployment line is full of well intentioned people that believe in hard work. Working hard is good, but working smartly will serve you better in the long run.

Cherish ever moment God allows you to spend with a loved one for it might well be your last.

Do not blindly put your trust in smart, educated men, or let them do the thinking for you. It is precisely these smart and educated men that keep mankind on the brink of chaos and extinction.

A college education is not a license you must acquire to think for yourself.

Tradition is a good thing, until it becomes an unbending obsession that must be maintained at all cost.

If you feel you cannot accomplish something, then don't even bother. Leave it to the guy who feels he can, because he is more likely to succeed.

When I look for talent, I look for the guy who believes 2 + 2 can equal 7, under the right circumstances.

All other things good, a husband and wife that can't or won't communicate with each other are no more; it's just a matter of time.

As a leader, remember that a whisper in the ear is far more productive than a bat to the back of the head.

If you have to be told how to properly treat another person, then your mother should have thought twice about kissing your father and saved us all the trouble.

The most intense feeling of happiness a person will ever experience comes from being in a state of love. Conversely, the loss of love, or of a loved one, is the most intense feeling of unhappiness one will ever experience; nothing else even comes close.

With few exceptions, if I want to do something, and I have the desire and means to do so, then I should not have to get permission from my government to do it.

Governments and lawyers are alike in that they both take a good concept and screw it up. As citizens, we are usually better off until one or the other enters the picture. Could one then draw the conclusion that the reason our government is so dysfunctional is because it consists of too many lawyers? Hmmm…I wonder.

If there is one thing that man has perfected since his conception, it is the art of denial.

Nothing brings more detriment to mankind than man's
undying determination to bring order to his surroundings.

Chaos breeds contempt for authority. Yet it
is that very contempt for authority that is
the breeding ground for great change.

The seriousness of a situation is in direct
proportion to your preparedness.

Speak to your young children as though you were speaking to yourself as a child, only with more authority, reason, and wisdom.

Be free enough to ride the wind, but grounded enough to surf the waves of reality without drowning.

I've noticed over the years that the most content and happy people are often those who have the least in the way of "things". They seem to be content with what little they have, for they have mastered the ability to find delight and happiness in the intangible. Perhaps they deceptively exist on a higher spiritual level than the rest of us.

If someone or something seems too good to be true, then it's probably a good idea to take a step back and reexamine the situation with less brain and more gut.

Ignorance is bliss…until it bites you square in the ass!

I seriously doubt if man can ever achieve a state of pure and enduring happiness. To be truly happy you must be content and I don't believe it is in man's nature to linger in a state of contentment. I pray that one day we will evolve to that point, though. In the meantime, however, all we can hope for is to live in moments of happiness as often as possible.

Question him, question her, and question it. Our ability to question our government, and our right to voice that question freely and loudly, is the bedrock of our democracy. When we are stopped from questioning or cease to question the actions and motives of our elected officials is when we begin to acquiesce and cede to totalitarian rule.

Be careful not to categorize and trivialize all actions or events based solely on your belief system. What is perceived as a little thing to you will almost certainly be realized as a significant event for someone else.

In the beginning, man's need to socialize was mainly for protection, as there was safety in numbers. Today, man's need to socialize seems to be purely a result of his higher need to belong...no matter the cost to his personal safety.

To be productive you must move…either your brain or your muscles. Of course, moving both in unison is always optimum.

The tongue can puncture the skin as deeply and efficiently as the sword. However, more easily healed is the wound from the sword.

A sedentary lifestyle gets you nowhere fast.

The depth of a person's thinking reflects
the maturity of his or her soul.

We "think" not because we can, but because we must...
to survive. It's very simple. Those who "think" survive
and flourish while those who don't wither and perish.

Pursuing a life of adventure is the key to achieving
personal fulfillment. Without adventure there
is no risk. Without risk there is no discovery.
And, without discovery there is no reward.

The difference between success and failure is that the successful person views the world around him/her as an opportunistic asset, not a liability that must be dealt with.

Those who govern without regard for the common man are destined to be forgotten. Those who do will be revered and fondly remembered in perpetuity.

The most allusive, formidable, and stubborn adversary you will ever face is yourself. Overcome the adversary within and the world is yours for the choosing.

The brain is nothing more than a three-pound pile of mush...until it is written upon with the pen of experience and learning.

I'd rather live a short life as an adventurous, inquisitive, and learned man, than a long life as an easily content, untraveled, and ignorant man.

The more broadly learned you become, the more you are capable of successfully adapting to your environment...and to that of others.

The person who easily gives up on others finds it easy to give up on himself or herself, as well.

We are all lost and found many times throughout our lives. The trick is to remain found longer than we remain lost.

The successful man is the one who is prepared and capable of reinventing himself to meet the needs of his environment.

Viewing oneself with reverence is greatly
preferred to viewing oneself with disdain.

The opinion you hold of yourself and your abilities
will largely determine your level of success or failure.

Learn as much as you can in as many different fields
of study as possible. This will greatly enhance your
chances of being secure in both mind and employment.

Generally speaking, love…and love will be given in return. Hate…and hate will be given in return. It's that simple.

Our ability to show indifference to those less fortunate is only overshadowed by our innate ability to inflict pain and agony on our fellow man.

The ability to transfer what you've learned to another person requires a dedicated effort on both the part of the learner and the learned. Perhaps that's the reason it rarely gets done.

Aspiring to be everything you can possibly dream
of becoming is what makes life worth living.

I feel sorry for those who ridicule others for dreaming,
but not as sorry as I feel for those who have their
dreams taken from them by such dreamless people.

I cannot think of anything in this world that
can so effortlessly and quickly unite people of all
backgrounds in total peace and harmony than
a good musical beat or an expertly crafted lyric.
If you don't believe me, just go to a concert.

Leaders nurture the talents of everyone under
their command, not just a select few of their
often myopic and ignorant choosing.

No one can ever force you to do what you do not want to
do. Even God doesn't interfere with your ability to choose
a particular course of action. Therefore, "choice" is always
yours and yours alone. So is victory or defeat. Letting
others decide your life for you is welcoming certain defeat.

If you are lost, do everyone a favor
and ask God for directions.

There are those who lead and those who
follow; the world needs both. But know this…
no one ever remembers the follower.

Fear is unknown to no one but the foolish and
timid. Fear of the unknown, and the willingness
of the brave to venture into it at their own peril,
has always been the impetus to great discovery and
change. God bless the brave and adventurous!

You can run from family, friends, responsibility,
and danger, but you can never run fast enough
or far enough to escape from yourself. Yet,
amazingly, people continue to try.

If you have a fear, face it head on. If it bites, bite it back...only harder.

The greatest, most rewarding moments in life are those that require you to push beyond your perceived limits and into the realization that you can do more than you ever imagined possible.

Life is like football. The safe bet is to grunt it out on the ground for a yard here and there. The real challenge and opportunity for success, though, comes from the person willing to take a chance and throw the long ball. That's what makes the game of life interesting, as well.

I prefer to die with my boots on, a hard earned sweat on my brow, and my wife and children by my side.

The little, bothersome things in life are like leeches; they latch on and drain you of your sustenance. If you don't learn to shake them off every now and then, they will accumulate and weaken you to the point that all else is impossible.

Leadership is for the brave. All others need not apply.

We can't possible know everything, but we better be damn sure we know more than our adversaries and competitors.

Perhaps the most arduous endeavor man will ever embark upon is the journey to discover his God-given purpose. Sadly, few even try. But, for those of us who actively pursue it, we can only hope to make the discovery while we still have time to make use of it. To do so requires us to put ourselves in as many places and situations as we possibly can. And, if we're lucky, our purpose will rise to the surface and grab us by the throat so that we might recognize it for what it is.

At the top of the food chain is Mother Nature, and she is bound and determined to never let us forget that.

The most frustrating position to be in is the one in which you feel you have no control as to the outcome.

We all have the ability to see others for what they are and ourselves for what we are not. Unfortunately, this is an ability many people choose to activate sparingly.

The propensity for war and destruction is in man's nature. This is the beast we have yet to tame.

Love isn't as much about the fulfillment of your needs and desires as it is about that of the person you love. The part of "love" that so many people struggle with is the realization that, at some point, you must either be there to patiently nurture the other person's talents, or be willing to let that person go…to be what he or she is destined to become.

No person is perfect. That's why God put us here…to work out our imperfections. If we were perfect in body, mind, and spirit, there would be no need for us to be here.

Don't let the beauty in life go by unnoticed. Make time every day to stop, look around, and appreciate the beautiful things in your life, and be thankful that God put them there for your pleasure and enjoyment.

The road less traveled is the road I prefer to be on,
for only then do I feel free enough to be me.

Your success as a leader depends less on your view from
the top than how others view you from the bottom. Your
people have to believe in your capabilities and respect
you as a person before they'll respect you as a leader.

We all strive to find the perfect job or occupation
that satisfies our talents, desires, and expectations.
That allusion, I'm convinced, only materializes
for a lucky few. The "perfect job" exists
mostly in the minds of ignorant fools.

Perhaps the most destructive words a leader
can utter are…me, myself, and I.

A man without honor and integrity is not a man at all. He
is merely a ball and chain upon the future of mankind.

Acknowledge and return the love you receive
often and sincerely, otherwise it will move on to
someone else who will pay it more attention.

Nothing as we know it moves without impetus.
Great leaders learn to apply the right amount
of impetus at precisely the right moment.

Few traits are as important to a leader as the ability to
interact with people on a sincere and personal level.

Seek out those who find friendship and value in you
for who you are as an individual, for I believe they are
there by God's design to assist you along your way.
Run from those that demand you be like them. They
are the devil's own and should be avoided at all cost.

Great leaders create an environment where employees can come to work and feel respected, valued, and an integral part of the team.

Laughter begets laughter. A smile begets a smile. A positive attitude begets action.

You know you've achieved absolute self-actualization when you've reached a point in life when you can be "yourself" in all situations and not an actor always trying to please an ever changing audience. Unless, of course, your chosen profession is acting.

A leader who truly believes he or she has all the answers leaves many unanswered questions.

As a leader, work hard, but work smartly…and let others see you doing it. However, don't ask others to do what you won't and don't expect others to do what you will.

Leave the past where it fell. Don't go back for it and drag it along with you or you'll never reach your potential while you're still young enough to enjoy the fruits of your labors.

Whether in battle or in business, nothing leads to failure faster than poor communications. Never assume others understand your orders or directions as well as you do.

The correlation between physical stature and one's ability to lead others lasts about 5 seconds.

A rock in a hard place is nothing more than a Stonehenge waiting to be erected.

When we sacrifice others for our own gain, we, in turn, sacrifice our spiritual growth tenfold.

Don't expect to be treated honestly and fairly if those words don't exist in your own dictionary.

It's ironic that the ones who know the most are the least to be sought out for their knowledge. And by this, I'm referring to the elderly. It's truly sad that the elderly are routinely cast aside and shunned by the youth of our nation. Do they not realize the value of this great and dwindling resource, and that with every passing day this untapped bank of knowledge is becoming irrevocably lost…forever, and ever, and ever?

About the Author

Jeffrey Wickey retired from the United States Air Force as a Senior Master Sergeant in April 2003 after proudly and faithfully serving his country for 21 years. While in the military he received numerous decorations to include four Meritorious Service Medals, four Commendation Medals, three Achievement Medals, and a Meritorious Unit Citation awarded by the United States Navy. He is currently a Senior Knowledge Management consultant at the Federal Energy Regulatory Commission (FERC) in Washington, D.C.

Born and raised in Sioux City, Iowa, he entered the United States Air Force in February 1982. As a career intelligence professional and Knowledge Management expert, he has worked as a military action officer and consultant at various institutions throughout the Washington, D.C. area to include the Pentagon, National Geospatial Intelligence Agency, Defense Intelligence Agency, Federal Bureau of Investigation, and Time Warner Cable. He has lived in several foreign countries and has traveled extensively for both work and pleasure.

He also maintains an undergraduate degree in Psychology from the University of Maryland, University College, and a post-graduate degree in Strategic Intelligence from the National Defense Intelligence College (formerly the Joint Military Intelligence College) in Washington, D.C.

He currently lives in Woodbridge, Virginia with his wife, Ellen, and has a son, JJ, and daughter, Laura, both of Virginia.